The Freedom in

Surrender

BY

DAVID MATTEO

The Freedom in Surrender

Copyright © 2020 by David Matteo

All rights reserved. No part of this publication may be reproduced, distributed, or transmitted in any form or by any means, including photocopying, recording, or other electronic or mechanical methods, without the prior written permission of the author, except in the case of brief quotations embodied in critical reviews and certain other noncommercial uses permitted by copyright law. For permission requests, write to the author, addressed "Attention: David Matteo" at the email address below.

ISBN: 978-1-7333675-5-4

Ordering Information:
Quantity sales. Special discounts are available on quantity purchases by churches, associations, and others. For details, contact the author at the address below.
Orders by U.S. trade bookstores and wholesalers. Please email David.K.Matteo@gmail.com.

To my sister Grace

The 'wild child' who tamed our hearts with a brave spirit;
I dedicate this to you.
You lived a life that was fearless in my eyes,
And even in death, you gave me the strength to not be afraid of my own.

I love you…and miss you every minute of each day.

Rest peacefully, until we are reunited.

Preface

What began as just a simple idea for a song, has now expanded into a collection of poems that capture the thoughts, emotions and triumphs during my spiritual awakening; which I have symbolically linked to the four classic elements – earth, water, air and fire.

The inspiration to write this collection was drawn from real life experiences and individuals who have been significant to my life, but also the desire to share the content which I believe God gave me to release. I never heard his voice more clearly then during this project and can honestly say that I was lost until I found the strength to first accept myself.

Over time, it took faith to believe that God would still love me despite my imperfections; but His love has proven to be stronger than any guilt, shame, regret or inadequacy I've ever felt. I pray that through relationship with Him, you also come to know this love and overall peace that He supplies. My hope is that you, the reader, can appreciate the sincerity and transparency of the work. It's quite difficult to face your demons alone, but I believe it takes more strength to be vulnerable and showcase them to the world.

Through this platform, if I could convey one point, it would be that you are unconditionally loved by God regardless of your struggle. We were not designed to be perfect and are not condemned for our sins, but we are reconciled back to Him by faith through relationship.

The freedom that I feel and experience today was only obtained after I surrendered control and adopted this belief; no longer punishing myself for every sin committed but rather accepting it as the very thing that makes me human.

Ultimately, I pray you follow your passions in pursuit of your purpose; where I believe lies your greatest source of fulfillment in this life.

May your path be abundantly blessed with peace, favor and love!

DAVID MATTEO

Earth

1

Foundation

Christ is my solid rock,

Who securely planted me on this turf
and keeps me grounded by faith.

Through sincere relationships, I've grown from the interactions of those alive and deceased,

Which have all proven essential for
my state of being,
Deeply connecting me to the concept
of what home truly means.

Core Strength

She stands tall and reigns

sovereign over all.
    Majestic in might as the
    protector of life.
    The complexity of her
designs are adored for its bounty
    and wonder;

Created by the divine to endure and sustain,
But her children bring pain that she cannot nurture.

    Mother nature has been patient in
    her torment,
    Suffering in silence as we consume
    her energy without fear of
    punishment;
    The result of this
consequence is sure to be violent;
    Her rage already evident by
the extreme force of the elements.

THE FREEDOM IN SURRENDER

We have destroyed her beauty for the sake of power and greed,
To the extent where now she desperately cries out and bleeds;
From depleted forestries, elevated heat and polluted seas,
To melting ice sheets, dead coral reefs and toxic air unsafe to breathe;

Those who fail to see have all been deceived…

To believe that we can abuse our planet and still survive is truly naïve.

The painful truth is that humans are the disease;
The cancer of this world;
the ulcer that's thrown natural equilibrium out of balance,
And now we are running out of time.

Our only recourse is to re-enforce that she's our most vital

                              resource;
Encourage the population to value
the significance of preservation;
Without which, there won't be a
place for procreation.

    Save her life… before it's too late,
        Our survival depends on it.

Fertile Ground

Lately it seems the spirit of death

is wildly rampant in the world;
All too soon consuming the lives of the innocent.

> Your earthly existence was transient,
> But your ethereal spirit is constantly revered by those you left behind.

The standard you set before us was that of excellence and integrity;
A testament to the strength of a true pioneer;
The matriarch who solidified and built our foundation on the value of trust.

> I'm beholden for your profound wisdom and favor;
> It was by design that our paths would cross and our stars align.

Your energy was radiant, an aura of
        light that is sorely missed,

But as I reminisce on the time we shared, I envision you in paradise like the Elysian Fields,
Crowned with glory and now protected by the hands of the Almighty.

    So I mourn not your death but
    celebrate your life and memory;
    Which will always reside in my
        heart and mind.
    Farewell my friend,
Until we convene next lifetime.

Chief Cornerstone

At night I've been restless;

Frightened that when I lay down to sleep, I won't wake up again.

As I recall the lives of friends who've passed prematurely,
I can't help but wonder if I'll share the same fate;

Albeit late,
I've realized my purpose now but question if there's still time;
Our most valuable commodity, seen as the true enemy of mankind;

It's inevitable that we are all appointed to meet an expected end. But death is what gives meaning to life
So I pray mine be extended,
With endurance and courage to

materialize my life's mission;
With strength to withstand the weight of any circumstance,
I know I'll remain stable with you as my balance;
The solid rock on whose foundation I stand firm.

By faith, my direction was revealed
And though accompanied with pressure, it initiated change;
The force that's corrected my posture to trust that you are always present;
Knowing that every expectation will be manifested
Because your power surpasses all restrictions;
You are not bound by my limitations.
Therefore, I'm convinced,
There's no reason to doubt.

Degree of Difficulty

It does exist;

No matter how hard they try to persuade you otherwise.
Be not deceived,
At the current rate, our demise *will* arrive sooner than we once believed. Sadly, our endless consumption of energy has limited our life expectancy.

Yet as we experience unprecedented natural disasters,
Those in power continually turn a blind eye, refusing to acknowledge the truth we all see;

IT'S ALL A LIE!

This war is sustained for the attainment of currency; with no regard for human lives;

> Meanwhile, our planet is on the brink of death,
> And they toy with us like a game that we remain in jeopardy;
> Unless we limit Earth's warming by at least a half degree,
> Failure to shift the course will result in imminent catastrophe.

They'll be no escape…
And the damage done will be irreversible.
Time is our most precious possession
> And *now* is our chance for redemption;
> Which should begin in each of us, fighting for the change we wish to see;

Awareness is ineffective unless accompanied by action…

> Are you a defender of life?

And if so, what position will you play to even the score?

The Illus-tree-ous

I convinced myself it was divine

timing for your early departure;
  That you fulfilled your purpose and
      therefore, returned home to the
            Father;
That was my only solace…
Death is most difficult for those left behind to feel the sting,
And you left us…suddenly… and without warning;
  Which pains me that I wasn't there
      when you were laid to rest;
  To not pay my respects and mourn
      your death,
  Is a moment I'll never get back and
      deeply regret.

But I'll *never* forget you, you are still alive in my thoughts today;
Our conversations empowered me with new perspectives unseen;

You inspired me to be the best and to never settle for mediocrity.
You told me that I was great…and I believed you,
Only because *you* were extraordinary;

The big brother I tried my best to emulate!
An innovative thinker and gifted writer;
A young prodigy wise beyond your years with a fool's sense of humor!
"Too cool for school" yet esteemed by our peers;
Far too advanced to ever be stuck in the rear;
And when you weren't around, your absence felt like we were worlds apart,
But time never seemed to lapse whenever you came back;
You were never *truly* gone.
And even at my worst, you never judged me,
Though at times I was out of order;
Instead, you gave sound reasoning

whenever I needed to plead my case.

You listened.
And understood me,
And I loved you for that.

> Words can't fully convey how
> special you were to me,
> But I pray this tribute brings justice
> to your memory;
> I will always regard you as supreme.

Seed of Mercy

I'm trapped in a vicious cycle and

can't break free;
Where I feel underserving of
sympathy because the issue is me,
And my *affinity* to be pleased…
Where in isolation, I've realized that
self-gratification no longer serves me
positively.

This stronghold drains my energy
because I'm full of rage,
Every day
From the state of my life;
Sorely vexed to deny myself the
attention I crave,
So, I tease myself in the face of sin,
only to quickly succumb to lust

again;
Steering opposite of the right direction, where pleasure turns into pain;
Hiding my face from your sight, until I eventually crawl back into your presence;
With the hope that you'll forgive my empty repentance,
Knowing that my disobedience was done with intent.

> I know that I'm guilty…and I know what I deserve,
> Yet you never pronounced a sentence…

Thank you for the gift of forgiveness.

> My spirit is at peace to know that even in weakness, I'm still a representation of you;

Destined to expand despite my shortcomings.
You created me with unlimited potential to overcome;
 And with your help, this habit will

be broken,
Once and for all.

Fruit of the Vine

There's no need to further question my life's direction,
> Though I'm afraid of where this truth may lead;

I can no longer stay hidden because
> I'm destined to shine;
> Equipped with lyrics and rhymes inspired from above,

I rain down with melodies from heaven with a voice that's bless-ed;
And a presence that's intrepid; a force to be seen by all generations,
Where my gifts will give birth to exciting new creations;
Ancient of days as a voice to the youth,
I'm an instrument of light, guiding

those lost to the ultimate truth;
    That He is love and rules in all sovereignty,
And because He is, then so am I;
    A prince of the Most High, in desperate search of my queen to be,
An African beauty like Imani Izzi;
    That specialty designed especially for me,
My sacred treasure more valuable than diamonds and rubies,
Who will compliment my life as well as complete me.
But He said I must do my part for my dreams to manifest,
Accept the call and trust in my heart that he'll provide the rest,
    Walk beside Him in faith, because I can't run anymore…
    There're souls attached to my decisions and I believe the story that was foretold,
    That I'm being shaped into a man of great influence;
Where others will be saved by the strength of my testimony,
And those I love will prosper once I

                        surrender completely,
I believe it…
Wholeheartedly,
So,
Here I am.

Hidden Jewels

In the most complex and intricate ways,
Through space, time and pressure;
Form treasures of spectacular variation;
Unique creations nestled deep inside our land and sea;
Possessing properties and vibrations of the energies absorbed within.
It was by fate you found me,
Where your power and influence have been proven instrument;
Beneficial in channeling inner strength to communicate and balance emotions effectively;
Challenges that once kept me anxious but now I remain centered,
With turquoise, amber, larimar and lava stone; I stand *TALL;*
Feeling spiritually grounded and connected to the place I call home.

The universe heard my pleas and supplied the answers with precious stones,
That enhance my courage and stimulate my self-confidence,
Never having to doubt who I am,
Or my purpose,

Ever again.

Nature's Cure

Sweet spirit,
 I marvel at your love for us;
  How wondrous is your habitation?
Lush vegetation concealed with abundant powers that heal,
 Where upon consumption, a therapeutic release can reveal true works of creativity;
The key that unlocks the doorway to higher consciousness and dispels the strain of negativity;
A comfort whose influence brings peace in time of confusion;
Apparent in my life at a time when I couldn't understand music clearly,
 Where despite best efforts, comprehension of theory eluded me;

I was frustrated…and ready to quit, to spare myself from further embarrassment,

But I was presented with a remedy;
A cure that promised to *'soothe the senses'*
And it was there that we were introduced.
Our first interaction was simply magic; excitingly euphoric and orgasmic,
The catalyst for a spiritual awakening where my gifts were set free,

A breakthrough of artistic expression emerging from the lower depths beneath;
Filling the void of emptiness and now I'm purposefully driven,
More than I've ever been,
To manifest every dream into reality.

I've attained so much strength…and power,
Whereby I create my surroundings with positivity *because* I believe,

That my mind is infinite
with possibilities, not bound by
limitations.
And though a temporary escape
from the chaos of this world,
I delight myself in your presence;

How you expose me to new
levels of insight,
Granting knowledge that
was never perceived before.
Now everyday I'm on the rise;
Falling deeper in love with the way
you make me feel…

Fearless!

DAVID MATTEO

Water

Emotions

The current wave of new experiences wash away the anxiety in my life,
    As my journey is directed from the source in unique rhythm.
    While healing old wounds of pain and becoming a reflection of love,
I realize there are things I cannot change but only accept;

    No matter the circumstance.

Erosion

It's still a mystery how you came

to me;
    Perhaps maybe a stroke of
      serendipity,
But what has come to be, I'm convinced was preordained because
    with one gaze,
    You unlocked my psyche;
Freed me from the chains of mental
    bondage and became a soul tie;

How is it that you excite and frighten me with every word you speak?
While so eloquently depositing seeds of vitality?

  I was stuck in a world of mundane
    until you changed the game;
  Never knew that you'd provide so

> much insight and wisdom;
> Multifaceted, you're like a crystal prism,
> Whose transparency shed light on the areas I tried to conceal.

Yet intently, you sensed my distress;
Then tore my defenses down and exposed my frailty;
Forcing me to confront my demons to facilitate self-healing.

> Through your strength, you made me acknowledge my weaknesses
> And I was scared…

Afraid to let anyone inside my space;
Intentionally sabotaging potential relationships based on fear
But you taught me that vulnerability is a risk, and necessary for growth;

> *So, I took the leap!*

And now… I've never felt more free!
FREE AT LAST!!!

No longer concerned with the labels
    of society but more of substance;
And in the simplest form, we are all stardust,
Fashioned in the Creator's imagination;
Dispersed as spiritual beings that are not cursed, but pro-creators of life filled with love,
And *that* love has no restrictions.

    Your creativity is magnificent;
With every aspect being so rich with depth;
And my life has been enriched with *you* in it.
You've been imprinted on my heart and will never be washed away,

This love is concrete.

S.O.S

The time has come for me to do what's right;
    His word I've neglected but still
        expect to hear his voice;
    Seems there's so many distractions
        around to make a choice,
    Especially when tempting thoughts
        consume my mind.

Above all, I just want Him to be pleased
And every second I waste, I'm on the decline;
Depreciating like an asset over time,
Confined in the dirt with the grit and grime,

    But there's only one way to be truly
        cleansed.
    The path has been made but I've

yet to pay the toll;
Afraid of what I'd meet at the end of
that road,
Afraid of negative critique if I
exposed my soul,

But I have nothing left to hide;

No longer afraid of the words I
speak, now that confidence is
soaring at its peak;
I'm high on love and know that
more than faith, He desires my
trust;
But I can't pretend that the weight
of sin is light;

It's frequency is heavy and vibrates
with a raging pulse;
A hypnotic trance that's seductive
where I lose all self-control…
Until sex ensues from the energy I
exude;
An insatiable hunger that's dying to
be fed.
Resistance proves ineffective when
trying to change on my own;

THE FREEDOM IN SURRENDER

I'm a disaster and so this is my last call of distress;
My only hope lies with you being the strength I lack;
The force that compels me back to you;
                Please rescue me soon.

The Best Stroke

This revelation came to me as an epiphany;
    I've been cruel towards you…
By never accepting the beauty in all
        that you are,
And the attempts to alter your state
    have only exposed my insecurity.
Please forgive me,
As I've realized those actions were superfluous;
Letting society dictate my perception of what measures a man;
But I am more than my exterior!
And any variation from the norm does *not* value me less.

    You were crafted by design to be
        unique,

Exclusively mine and like you, there
is no other;
You are a part of my individuality
and there's no reason to be
ashamed…

So, Arise!

You are truly an aesthetic form of art!
Capable and fully strong to function as God intended!

There's no need to be afraid;
I'll never put you through that pain again,

I promise.

Water under the Bridge

I miss you;

Though my pride is resistant to admit it.

> It angers me that I bared my soul for you;
> Revealing my darkest fears and exposing my vulnerabilities;
> Only to be embarrassed and covered by your blanket of deceit.

Maybe I divulged too much prematurely;
An excuse I tell myself to justify your actions lately;

Did I scare you off?

Because honestly, I felt a true connection with you,
A feeling I presumed was mutual;

Never before had the desire been so strong
Where I could barely sleep, dreaming of the love we'd make;
Overstimulated simply by the thought of the sensation,
I could hardly wait!

I offered you my complete trust because I felt special;
Finally, comfortable to be seen,
And then you disappeared;

Abandoned me to be left alone with my thoughts,
Drowning in the sea of uncertainty, accompanied with memories of your sweet sorrow.
And now I feel foolish for being manipulated;
Which I've never tolerated from

anyone before you.

> Why did you do this to me?

Reluctantly, I let my guard down because I thought you were worth the risk;

> A feat that took everything within me to accomplish
> But I guess I was mistaken;

It's obvious you didn't want me the way I wanted you;
And I refuse to remain in pain so I elect to take this stance;
To sever all ties, so I can slowly mend my brokenness…

> Goodbye.

Ti-dal Wave

It's unfortunate at times…

That those close to you never seem to recognize your value;
Being constantly overlooked, leading you to question your self-worth,
But I implore you never change.

Though it be difficult for them to acknowledge the love you demonstrate,
You require no validation,
Because the purity of your deeds are evident;

Selflessly enduring the burdens of

others, yet somehow remaining
stoic;
With a posh fashion style and keen
eye for classic vintage,
You are a timeless wonder in an
aging world!

    Gifted with the innate capacity to
                        lead by virtue;
A commitment that often leaves you
                    misunderstood and
                      underappreciated,
But your sacrifices have not been in
vain.

You've been chosen and called for a
                higher purpose;
   Not to be conformed by the lower
           standards of this world.
              You've been set apart,
And very few understand the depth
   that's derived from your worship;
          And why you're guarded,
But it's obvious our connection was
by no mistake.

    He aligned our paths so I would

understand the relevance of trust;
And by example, your life has been
a true testament,
Of what it means to trust Him even
in the face of doubt...

My belief was solidified because of you.

Like water, you are a source of life
that sustains me;
Where I'm lost in your ocean and
drawn by the strength your
gravitational pull;

Like a triad of Earth, Moon and Sun,
We are one through the Father, Son and Holy Spirit.
My life would be empty without you;
And to my heart, you will always have the key,

Forever.

Liquid Courage

I don't want to hide this from you anymore;
> There are parts of my life I kept hidden because I knew you wouldn't understand
>> But at this point,

God has given me so much clarity as to who I am and what I'm meant to be;

Where I've never felt more complete
> until I accepted my sexuality;

Finally admitting that my dual preference is only a part of my individuality.

I know its unorthodox for you to

accept,
But I can no longer deny or repress the emotions I feel because the sentiments *are* real.

I wish the bond between us was stronger, where I'd feel comfortable confessing this to you,
But I was fearful you wouldn't view me the same;
Afraid that I'd bring shame to our family, when all I wanted to do was to honor you.

For years your neglect made me resentful, although I craved your presence;
I needed your guidance...
But for so long, I felt lost inside;
Crying out for you to help me rationalize my identity,
But in my loneliness is where God spoke to me.

I desired intimacy and asked Him to lead me, even in my iniquity,
And He answered with an

opportunity that I recently explored.
And through that encounter, I emerged empowered;
No longer weak but more secure in my abilities;
Confident with a better sense of realization;
Dismissing the fallacy of what I perceived was truth.

> What I need now, is for you to understand that these experiences shape who I am;
> But they don't define me.

I'm still your son and I still love you beyond capacity;
I'm surpassing boundaries to heights I never thought I'd reach

> And in time,

You'll see that each moment propels me to my ultimate destiny;
To live a life I can be proud of; a life of purpose,

One where I hope you'll truly be
proud of me.

Wavering

I feel so timorous;

My body shaken to the core because yesterday, I received what I prayed for;
The freedom to engage in illicit relations but now I'm plagued with second thoughts;
Nervous in perpetual trepidation for the retribution that I expect to be wroth.

    I can't seem to win this battle;
I've been at war for ages and have no energy to fight,
The internal struggle of the mind where I have no control to do what's right…

I have nothing left.

THE FREEDOM IN SURRENDER

Bereft of hope, I relentlessly sought you, seeking safety from the dangers of self-infliction;
Away from destructive thoughts of ill intent, that whisper there's no escaping consequence…

> But constant conviction is my affliction;
> Wrestling with the potential repercussion of my decisions;
> Do I continue to satisfy the flesh and bask in this painful pleasure,
> Or deny desire to strive for a higher measure?

What do I choose?

Because for years I tried to ignore this attraction you abhorred
But it wouldn't be denied;
> All attempts to keep it hidden only brought it closer to the forefront;
> And this time,
> When it knocked on my door, I let it in;

Succumbing to that lustful hunger I felt within,
Where every inch of my anatomy was explored with intense passion;
Each touch generating a new spark of ecstasy,
Exciting every nerve cell deep inside and high above,
Lost in euphoria, submerged with no wish to be found.

It felt true…

But how irony abounds;
That even in my sinful state, I believe He favors me every day;
Being liberated to share and receive love, even though I feel trapped by guilt.
Is this perception real?
Or am I justifying my actions to put my mind at ease?
I want to trust my instincts that led me to this sense of liberty

But where am I?

THE FREEDOM IN SURRENDER

All is Well

As the tears stream down my face,
I may appear to weep in
response to pain and distress;
Maybe perceived as weak
from sorrow too fierce to suppress;
But actually, it's quite the contrary.
They shed from a state of reverence;
Esteem in humble gratitude for the condition of my life;
Being supplied with favor, acceptance and above all, freedom!

I anticipate our reunions;
All for the chance to exist in
your presence again;
Where I'm cleansed in the
still of silence, unable to speak by
the weight of your glory.

It's astounding how you hear my unspoken language,
Even when I can't articulate emotions through words.
But you see past that, and feel the intentions of my heart;

>That can finally say I love you;
>Fervently,
>And without expectation;
>Fully comprehending the
>depth of grace unmerited;
>Which in turn makes me
>question,
>Why me?

>What's so special about me?

Pray for Rain

Why are *we* the recipients of

extreme persecution,
> When it seems no other race has been targeted more than us?
> We are an endangered species, hunted for the sole purpose of eradication;

Trapped in a proverbial jungle where our predecessors endured constant resistance,
> All for our basic right just to be deemed human.

They want our history erased;
To feed us their lies and conceal the truth,
That we are descendants of African royalties;
Our veins rich from the blood of ancient dynasties,
Created as celestial beings, gifted with supernatural power that can't be contained.

We were born free… and yet our
freedom came at great cost.

Against our will, we were stolen from
our native land and auctioned as
property;
Deliberately withheld from education
to keep us ignorant,
Therefore, dependent on charity to
uphold their fallacy of superiority.
Our ancestors were tortured,
mutilated and killed with no regard
for life;
Victims of unfathomable crimes for
which there can be no recompense.

Even in destitution,
We paid everything for the
progression of our oppressors yet
received nothing in return;
But further destruction from the
generations that followed;
Continuing their perpetual cycle of
violence and hatred.

Then they brand us 'insane' when we
refuse to pledge allegiance for a
country that doesn't protect us…

The 'just us' system is *NOT* for all;
but catered only to the majority that
promotes racial division.

How can we be united when we're
not even considered equal?

A harsh reality to admit,
But our spirit has always been
resilient in the face of adversity.

AND SO WE MUST CONTINUE
THE FIGHT!
So that the sacrifices made before us
were not futile;

Every individual contributes to the
collective body and being unified is
where we draw our strength!

Believe in us,
Because I believe in each of you.
Together, we *can* shift the course and
change our story.

Air

Communicaton

Through intimate relationship,
have I heard you speak with clarity in silence;
> Offering words of forgiveness and
> visions that guide my path.
> Through transparency, will I attempt
> to empower the world;
> For others to see that they're not
> alone in their struggle…

But to encourage them to believe that with you, *nothing* is impossible!
All that's required is an ear to listen,
And the courage to follow your intuition and *ACT!*

> Don't be afraid to trust your inner voice.

3-way Call

Lonely days and sleepless nights had become the routine of my life;
Feeling void of touch with a heart of stone, I found comfort in being alone;
Solace in solitude, I took refuge from the multitude;
  No longer seeking favor among men but favor from Him,
  Because when I placed my trust in them, it was all to my detriment;
  Deep in despair did I descend;
  Disoriented from chasing the American dream but in reality, I was empty;
Clocking eight each day for the almighty dollar
Only to waste time building someone else's wealth.

  There had to be more in store;
  I refused to believe that I'd reached the extent;
  And in my hour of need is when you dialed my number;

THE FREEDOM IN SURRENDER

Where I experienced a spiritual
phenomenon that was beyond words;
The first time I ever felt we
conversed!
A sense of clarity from connection
with universal energy,
Expressed in numerology by the
number three, thrice;
Confirmation that my supplication
was heard clearly!
My ascended master, the Holy
Trinity, sends a message to balance
mind, body, and spirit;
And now I believe more than ever
that my life has purpose;
To inspire humanity with my artistry
where His vision will be made
apparent;
In my walk that now has new
direction and a clear path;
That enables me to speak to my
situations boldly,
And to stand strong in the face of
adversity, with confidence!

I won't run away;
I'll fulfill my current assignment and
remain still;
And until you order my next move,
I'll listen carefully
And hold on.

A Sweet Sound

I love when you speak,

    Because it validates the authenticity
                  of our connection;
    Which is not always necessarily
    "heard" but the message is clearly
                          received;
Either through a person, intuition or
a vision;
Your methods always confirm the
things I've sought from you in prayer.
    During moments of introspection, I
        analyzed my emotions and fears;
            Acknowledged your signs and
        adjusted my actions accordingly;
    Finally placing my faith in motion!
    Exploration had been stalled long
                              enough;
And though contrary to your word, I
        had to know for myself;

In order for me to understand who I
truly am!
But since that day, I've had feelings
of regret;
Believing my conduct will never be
forgiven,

But you sent a messenger through my
dream one day!
Who relayed that though the wages
of sin is death, I've been pardoned by
grace;
The most mellifluous expression of
mercy I've ever heard…
That makes my heart scream with a
resounding voice to simply say,

          THANK YOU!!!

No Pressure

No one can choose the family they're born into,
  Yet I couldn't have asked for a better selection;
    Surrounded by intellectuals of all professions;
  I adore being connected to this tree!
And having you as my matriarch;
Where recently we sat down to discuss extending the branches;
Which made me reflect on the significance of a name;
How culture, creativity, individuality and influence are attained from our ancestors;
  All attributes embodied in that which we are called;
  Where in the distant past, I spent my time travelling through constellations;
Dancing amongst the stars until conception gave me physical form;
Being born unto two of the most beautiful humans in the world
As the third and only male, I often questioned If I'd ever find 'the one'?

> But you consoled me with reassurance, like only a mother's clairvoyance could;
> And in that second, all doubt was cast aside with a smile;
> Knowing that whether I'm blessed to procreate or not, *you* are satisfied.

But I believe God!

And await my presents to be gifted;
Where through birth, I hope to present new entities into Earth;
Divine representations to continue our lineage and honor our legacy;
Being nurtured in love through wisdom and freedom;
Who will breathe life, just as it was given to me…

> When it's the right time.

With a Voice of Triumph

It's innate within you to educate;
> From an early age, you strongly
> desired to learn with avidity;

An honorable trait most consistent in
> your family,

Whose zeal for knowledge and truth
has shaped the man you've become
> today.

Inquisitive by nature, you've become
quite the explorer of information;
A savant who extricated the mental
block of my creative thoughts
By suggesting I unleash control and
accept new ideas;

THE FREEDOM IN SURRENDER

To ignore structure and remove
restraint, even if the concepts sound
weird;

                Don't hold back…

And with that notion, you freed my
mind to flow unrestricted;
Where my poetry has flourished from
the influence of your wisdom;
Words dance to a beat and now I
write in a different rhythm;
Articulating the measure of my
emotions with distinct precision.

       Thanks to candid context, I've
            produced deeper content;
Where profound lyrics have detailed
                my life experience;
   It feels the most authentic and it
          finally makes sense;
Expressing the extent of my vision
                with full clarity.
              It's important to me;
As I realize how significant words
                    can be
               To evoke change.

Who knows where this road will lead?
But it's exciting to think a part of me
   can potentially live beyond this life;

As an aid used to motivate and
inspire future generations.
Through music, I found the
confidence to believe in my voice;
Thank you for showing me the
strength of my mind!

Lung Restriction

I'll admit it…
 I'm selfish.
Though it's never my intention to be;
To demand everything from you
while offering nothing in return…

Is it wrong to ask you to forgive me?

For neglecting to spend time with
you then choosing my availability?
There's nothing on my schedule
more important than you,
Yet you're allotted only a small
fraction of my time;
The majority wasted on meaningless
pursuits that ultimately keep me
distracted;

Knowing full well that I need to
submit but intimidated by the
commitment;
Focusing on everything I'd lose
instead of what I'd gain.

> But to blame my absence on 'human
> nature' is no excuse for attending to
> the world;
> That's not what you deserve;
> Nor does it encapsulate my true
> emotions towards you.

You are *so* necessary to me;
Not only for granting me the life I
live;
But surrounding me with love that
only your spirit can provide;
Being replete with joy!

> But it's time my actions coincide with
> my words.
> Please give me the chance to correct
> my mistakes;
> It's my fault that these limitations
> even exist in the first place.

I know what must be done;
I need to re-dedicate myself to
obedience;
So that I can remove the blockage of
all negative traits,

THE FREEDOM IN SURRENDER

And just,
Breathe.

DAVID MATTEO

First Breath

Did you ever think our paths would
have crossed like this?
                      Neither did I…

But I always believed my life could
change forever in an instant;
And through this experience, that
belief has proved evident.

  Decisions I neglected to make in the
        past kept me from truly living;
  But by faith I found my way, and the
    strength to endure along my quest.
With my sight set on new
explorations; it was there I found
you,
A familiar face in a strange land,
A coincidental occurrence, seemingly
orchestrated by the hands of fate;
Where our serendipitous rendezvous
was a moment I'll always treasure;
  An alluring night filled with pleasure
        underneath the midnight sun;

That commenced with conversations
of aspiring dreams, poetry and
moments of lucidity;
There I sat, mesmerized by the
mystique in the air that surrounded
us;
Soon aroused by the thoughts of
scandalous behavior,
It was *that* moment your eyes
confirmed what we both desired.
You made the first move and I
followed your lead;

Like a sage skilled in the art of
seduction,
Your instruction was succeeded with
our bodies unveiled;
Creating the ideal atmosphere for
sexual synergy that was out of this
world!
Each touch explosive with electricity;
stimulating every erogenous zone on
my body;
It was transcendent;
Unlike anything I've ever experienced
before;
And for the first time sex was
unrestricted;
Animalistic where I re-discovered my
dominance;
Passionate aggression I forgot even
existed until then!

I missed that…

But you showed me those feelings
never left my side;
I've been revived!
Where I've never felt more alive
Than with you!

Jersey Flow

I never imagined our friendship

would have evolved into this;
   One built on trust and vulnerability;
   A dynamic noticeably present in that
              of a patient and therapist.
Well I feel safe in the space we've
established;
A genuine comradery filled with
laughter and encouragement,
Motivation and enlightenment,
Where our discussions have been
invaluable; integral in my progression
of independence!
  There is *power* in your voice and *weight*
                 to your words;
    That when you speak, you compel
                others to action!
            Being well respected,
You're an exceptional leader who by
example, makes following direction
                   effortless;

And it's by this measure that you
inspire others to a higher merit;
By recognizing value and nurturing
skill to increase the echelon of our
personnel;

        You care for us, personally;
An admirable trait that makes you
                      auspicious;
    For your willingness to fight and
protect those you love, who may not
           exhibit the same strength.
To us, you are irreplaceable;
A sophisticated treasure, with
abundant creativity and an epicurean
palate;
Whereby we're fed by your
knowledge and expertise in the
facilitation of our growth!

Your presence has changed the
trajectory of my life;
And what a guiding light you've been
on my path to illumination;
The epitome of a gold standard!

Just Say the Word

There appears to be a recurring
theme of you persistent in my
dreams;
Which makes me question,
Whether your presence should be
perceived as figurative or literal?
    I'm inclined to think the latter;
    And believe your existence in this
        matter is not by coincidence!

You will be mine;
There's no other way to rationalize
this magnetic attraction I feel.
    All the while, I've been patiently
        waiting for a sign;
    Any indication from you that
    corroborates the visions I've seen;
Wherein our kiss was highly amorous
        and I exultant!
From the culmination of years trying
        to solicit your affection!

DAVID MATTEO

I'm dying to feel your touch,
And to lie next to you at the end of each day;
But I'm tired of not waking up to this truth;

                We need to talk…

Zephyr Breeze

My spirit is calm, gently resting on a plane of weightlessness;
As peace has subsided the turbulence of anxiety that made me feel submerged.
But I've reached the surface through transparency;
And with all my demons exposed, it was difficult to see the disappointment in your eyes;
But your stride to understand was more than I expected; a pleasant surprise!
To hear you listen and not judge, Then offer guidance in love, touched my heart in a very special way,
When honestly from the start, I expected an abrupt end.

But you didn't abandon me…

    And now I desire to cleave to you more than ever before;
Believing in our potential and the strength of our bond,
To be what I always knew it could be…
The way I always wanted *us* to be…
Close;
Confident to approach you with any circumstance, knowing that your love would still be present.
Because in the past, there were moments of uncertainty but this instance proves definite;

    That without question, our relationship can be stout…
        If you want it to be.
But look at me, I feel liberated!
Overwhelmed in the freedom to personally engage anyone I choose;
And I know you don't approve
And I'll always respect your stance;
But at this juncture, we've been given the opportunity to enhance our weakened alliance;

    And if it can be improved, even in the slightest;
    I believe it's worth the fight…

        Don't you?

THE FREEDOM IN SURRENDER

DAVID MATTEO

Fire

Passion

I'm free!
Detached from all feelings of guilt
and shame;
Reaching new heights of greater self-
awareness
Where I've never felt more powerful
in my entire life!
    Driven by desire, this leading force
        brought me to this crossroad;
            To either decline or thrive;
                To live or die…
            And I choose life!
Being open to all it has to offer.
And now here I stand; confident with
nothing left to hide;

Come see what I mean…

Burnt Out

This was only supposed to be temporary;
But this alternative solution of self-gratification
Has potentially caused permanent damage;
A form of prevention I *thought* was safe,
But whose action has triggered unforeseen casualty;
Derived from insecurities developed as a teen, I was subjected to ridicule relentlessly;
    Everything from being shamed for my heritage and dark skin,
    To not being masculine, enough;
Emasculated to the full extent, I was convinced I'd never meet expectation,
So I learned to satisfy my own needs;
Being gratified in my sexual interests solely
Where initially, it was riveting!

THE FREEDOM IN SURRENDER

        Until feeling that release became a dependency...
        More like a replacement;

Relying on the orgasmic sensation from masturbation to please me
Instead of seeking that comfort from another;
Avoiding all contact from the fear of performance anxiety,
While quietly shedding tears of frustration out of desperation just to be touched;
Some kind of physical stimulation from something other than my own hand
    Because I've been desensitized from this addiction;
    The result of abusing my body from the influence of pornography
Where now I find it hard to connect;

I'm exhausted...

And I want to break free,
But I'm hooked on the feeling that these endorphins bring;
Euphoric highs that entice explicit expression of sex sublime!
        But if that were true,
    Why do I still feel empty inside?

I know now that it's time to leave this behavior at the door and vacate,

So that I can finally let someone in.

Spark My Interest

I didn't expect this to happen,

> At all;
> Especially not after just one phone call;

But our conversation was so deep, it was full of intrigue;
Fascinating it didn't take long for you to gain my trust;
To prematurely disclose everything about me voluntarily,
Speaks to the level of comfort I initially felt.

Where you been hiding all this time?

Apparently, out of my sight
But now that you're here, I don't want you to leave;

Your presence is refreshing;
reminiscent to the first bloom of
Spring;
Budding with excitement and
possibilities that a new cycle can
often bring!

> At this stage, I can't deny,
> I actually have butterflies!
> All from the anticipation to make
> your acquaintance!
> Because you certainly captured my
> attention, by the sight of your
> unmentionables…

Where soon, I foresee a synergy;
As involuntary reactions visit
frequently and I'd love for you to
stay.
Let's discuss our arrangements at a
specified time and date;

Don't be late!

Hot Topic

Here's a proposition;
Suppose I said I'd like another to join our bed;
A single individual with mutual interest to explore a ménage á trois;
An experience we dare not miss;
To this, would you grant consideration?

Exhilaration rages from the expectation of a supplemental body,
Because to the conventional style of copulation, I've grown blunt.
Let's push our drive to the limit and get lost; ignoring the constructs of sexual boundaries!

I'm secure in what I feel;
To admit there's appeal on opposite ends of the spectrum;
A dichotomy of attraction equally desired on multiple levels;
And now I wanna explore *every* position…

Ranked from the slightest to the
extreme;
Where currently my soldier is at ease,
yet prepped for full a strike on your
command;

Ready to exert supreme power in
dominance, then yield in humble and
obedient submission…
Take me as your prisoner;
And with commanding authority, I'll
release full control of my body;
Permitting access to all areas once
restricted,
                Where upon entrance,
Allow him to satiate my hunger with
the force of his aggression,
As I consume the dark void between
your space;
Exploring the infinite depth of
mystery contained within this black
hole;
Savoring every moment of bliss that
brings me closer to the light!
Say you'll accompany me, and
sojourn into the unknown of this
forbidden realm;
This ship will only sail with you at the
helm and I'm ready to dive in…
You on board?

Boiling Point

I never pictured this in my wildest

dreams;
    That someone who looks like you
Would ever be interested in someone
                  like me;
But when we met, you were honestly
not what I expected;
Your photograph didn't do you
justice
By hiding the substance of all the
essential parts that matter;
But the science of this chemistry
couldn't be explained by mere physics
alone,
    Though your flawless physique left
                  me astonished
    And weak to be in the presence of a
              modern day Adonis;

Approaching me statuesque, with a
broad chest and toned build;
Apparently, destined to win any
contest by conquest
And as such, I surrender control and
admit defeat;
That it was hard just to summon the
courage to speak;
Being under the influence, anxious
from the overflow of mounting
pressure;
Meanwhile, trying not to measure the
size of your visible print in my
head…

Now all I can think about is how
your lips feel pressed against mine;
How you've sparked the flame for
this fire we made,
Awaiting the day to sample a taste of
your intricate design as our bodies
blend;
Moving to the beat of your rhythm in
perfect harmony.
So if you wanna score,
Lead me to your place and I'll follow
your direction,
But before we leave, make sure you
have protection;

This could get violent…

Shots Fired

So let me get this straight

    Because this must be some kind of
                                joke;
So,

Because I called you out through text,
For standing me up a *second* time with
          no remorse after the first,
              Makes me deserve your worst
                      behavior?
You actually have the nerve
To threaten me with confrontation,
When I warned you I wouldn't
tolerate this type of conduct;
Not after you've betrayed my trust on
multiple occasions,
Proving your disloyalty;
 Though you swear to me you've been
                nothing but faithful;
    But from what I see, that would be
                foolish to believe
    Because lately you've been distant;

Your signs are cryptic where I can't
decipher your intentions;
Your eyes express interest but your
actions say different
And it's *this* inconsistent pattern that
I can't get down with,

Because I never know what you're up
to,
Or where I stand;
Whether I'm just a pawn in your
clever game of chess
Or the last bullet aimed for your
heart,
Like a lethal round of Russian
roulette.
Am I worth the risk?

Because the revolving issues we have
all center around your lack of
commitment;
With the point being
I need you to focus on *me* in order to
feel protected;
So that when I'm hit with thoughts of
momentary doubt,
I'll know I'm covered.

Dim the Lights

The shows about to begin;

And it seems this little tease of yours
was just a preview;
A sneaky interlude of discreet
exhibition before our featured
presentation;
How fitting this surge of spontaneity
to occur in this location;
Surrounded by darkness and unseen
by wandering eyes.

The coast was clear,
And the trail you embarked on was
bold;
Beginning with a sweet caress of my
fingertips that led to our hands
united;
Conjoined as one, I could feel your
pulse reverberate;

Almost to the sound of my heartbeat,
Where this thrilling suspense had me on the edge of my seat!
    Anxious, yet exhilarated as you penetrated my barrier by force;
Being completely outside my comfort zone but an act I dared to permit;
And although reluctant, I'm glad you persisted;

The panic of being discovered in public,
Was quickly overshadowed by *ALL* the attention you gave me in private;

A warm, rhythmic and sensual salute enveloped by your lips,
So soft that I had to cease before an untimely outburst...
Needless to say, I could hardly keep my focus;
And now I'm curious to see what else you have in store...

    Care to meet for an encore?

Heated Debate

The time has come for you to

decide;
 If you wanna be single, then leave…
 There's no need for us to be partners
  When I already feel isolated in your company;

And with each day that we cohabitate,
It becomes increasingly clear you don't *truly* love me.

You can't;

Not when you lash out with verbal attacks that are passive aggressive;
Refusing to accept your anger as a result of your own insecurities;

Yet I'm expected to be content with the smidgen of affection you've shown me,
When all I've done is sacrifice everything just to make you happy.

But you aren't...

And it drains my strength to even try to pretend;
Like you're *not* emotionally absent with one foot outside the door,
But I won't reside here being dissatisfied;
Nor will I continue to compromise my sanity
To occupy a space with someone who hates me.

You can't deny it...

You resent me for past behavior that you can't focus on the present;
Placing the blame on everyone except where it lies...
But the truth is you don't trust me;
The obvious culprit for our severed connection
But at this point, separation seems best;
As I doubt this relationship will ever get any better;

THE FREEDOM IN SURRENDER

I have nothing further to give…but
stand to gain so much more from
losing you;
I deserve to be loved;
And to have that love reciprocated in
the same manner in which it's given;

I know it exists,

And I *will* find it without you;
A discovery that's been long overdue
To finally bring this cold war to an
end.

Glimpse into a Flame

Didn't seem that long ago
  When I stepped foot through those doors;
    Feeling shut out from the world;
    Broken in spirit and yearning to be restored;
    Unsure of life's direction and lost at my core;
    Somehow I found myself here from the options I explored;

He led me to you, the woman I've been searching for;

THE FREEDOM IN SURRENDER

I knew for sure the first moment our eyes connected,
We were destined to align;
The push was undeniably mesmeric, you *had* to have felt the pull;
From a force so strong, it stopped my heart with just one look;
A heavenly sight to behold as you slowly entered the room;
Commanding the worship from the believers that surrounded us;
Your radiant skin and golden locs crowned were indicative of your majesty;
A queen poised in grace, appointed to dominate and rule;
Bringing this royal kingdom under subjection from your reign of fire.
My body was set ablaze as I stood there frozen;
Spellbound by your smile and alluring scent; helplessly concupiscent from this enchantment;
But sadly to my disappointment, you declined my advancements,

Twice!

When I was certain the first attempt would have surely sufficed
But perhaps the third time's the charm;

Though my suspicion tells me this
signal is merely a false alarm;

>Are you *truly* disinterested or just
committed to another?

While it appears your level of
indifference is deliberate,
I sense through intuition that my
presence has captured your attention;

>Dare I speak the truth?

Because God gave me insight
through a dream;
With you

>Waiting on me to take the lead with
my approach;
But maybe that signified you waiting
on me, to follow you to God…
Either way, let's not waste another
second if you feel the same;
Just give me a minute of your time.

Trial by Fire

You can't hide forever...

Nor silence the cries or pain of the innocent;
 For all too soon, your sin will expose your secrets.

My heart laments for all the victims who've suffered at the hands of sexual abuse;
 Those subjugated under control by predators who manipulate and prey on the weak;
These criminals have escaped persecution from the lack of courage to speak;
Hoping that you internalize the hurt;
To quietly conceal the details of their detestable deeds,

But free speech shall not be suppressed!

By full disclosure, do we highlight the frequency of this injustice;
Through open protest, is the collective voice finally being heard;
One of the crucial steps in bringing accountability to the guilty!
Bring them forth to stand trial and demand retribution for the afflicted!

Trauma is always painful to revisit,
But I believe we overcome by the word of our testimony;
An effort that requires great strength but can also yield great triumph!

And to my brave soldiers:
I pray for closure to all your open wounds;
Healing from the emotional and physical scars that's been inflicted upon you;
Trust me,
You are not alone…

.

Acknowledgements

      First, I would like to give honor to God, my Creator and Heavenly Father who is the source of my life. You supply my every need and I would be nothing without your presence. By grace, you have blessed me with all that I hold dear; and every day my faith is strengthened in you through our relationship. Thank you for your love and acceptance; for peace and understanding of who I am and my purpose in you.

      I would also like to give honor to my parents; who throughout the years, have sacrificed so much to provide a better life for our family. Words cannot express how much I love you. Thank you for your wisdom, your guidance and encouragement; for always believing in our potential and rearing us with Godly compassion. It's been by your great example that I've learned how to love.

To my sister, thank you for loving and supporting me; for setting me straight like only an older sibling can! (smile). You've always been a great source of strength and I couldn't imagine living this life without you! Your distinct creativity has truly paved the way for your art to flourish and it's only a matter of time before it's recognized on a global scale…period! I love you!

To all my family and friends, thank you for the support you've shown and continue to provide. I would not be who I am without you!

www.ingramcontent.com/pod-product-compliance
Lightning Source LLC
Chambersburg PA
CBHW052101070526
44584CB00017B/2290